Mary Jones, Diane Fellowes-Freeman and Michael Smyth

Cambridge Checkpoint

Science

Challenge Workbook

8

CAMBRIDGE
UNIVERSITY PRESS

University Printing House, Cambridge CB2 8BS, United Kingdom

One Liberty Plaza, 20th Floor, New York, NY 10006, USA

477 Williamstown Road, Port Melbourne, VIC 3207, Australia

314–321, 3rd Floor, Plot 3, Splendor Forum, Jasola District Centre,
New Delhi – 110025, India

79 Anson Road, #06–04/06, Singapore 079906

Cambridge University Press is part of the University of Cambridge.

It furthers the University's mission by disseminating knowledge in the pursuit of
education, learning and research at the highest international levels of excellence.

www.cambridge.org
Information on this title: www.cambridge.org/9781316637234 (Paperback)

© Cambridge University Press 2017

First published 2017

20 19 18 17 16 15 14 13 12 11 10 9 8 7 6 5 4

Printed in Great Britain by CPI Group (UK) Ltd, Croydon CR0 4YY

A catalogue record for this publication is available from the British Library

ISBN 978-1-316-63723-4 Paperback

Produced for Cambridge University Press by White-Thomson Publishing
www.wtpub.co.uk
Editor: Rachel Minay
Designer: Dan Prescott

All Checkpoint-style questions and sample answers within this workbook are written by
the authors.

Acknowledgements

The authors and publishers acknowledge the following sources for photographs:

Cover Pal Hermansen/Steve Bloom Images /Alamy Stock Photo

....

Contents

Introduction

Welcome to the Cambridge Checkpoint Science Challenge Workbook 8

The Cambridge Checkpoint Science course covers the Cambridge Secondary 1 Science curriculum framework. The course is divided into three stages: 7, 8 and 9.

You should use this Challenge Workbook with Coursebook 8 and Workbook 8. The tasks in this Challenge Workbook will help you to develop and extend your skills and understanding in science. This workbook is offered as an extension to the main curriculum and therefore it does not cover all the curriculum framework content for this stage.

The tasks will challenge you with scientific enquiry skills, such as planning investigations, interpreting and analysing results, forming conclusions and discussing them.

They will also challenge you to **apply** your knowledge to answer questions that you have not seen before, rather than just recall that knowledge.

If you get stuck with a task:

Read the question again and look carefully at any diagrams, to find any clues.

Think carefully about what you already know **and** how you can use it in the answer.

Look up any words you do not understand in the glossary at the back of the Checkpoint Science Coursebook, or in your dictionary.

Read through the matching section in the Coursebook. Look carefully at the diagrams there too.

Check the reference section at the back of the Coursebook. There is a lot of useful information there.

Introducing the learners

Nor   Amal   Sam

Anna   Elsa   Jon

Unit 1 Plants

1.1 Turning an idea into a question that can be tested

This challenge task relates to **1.3 Investigating photosynthesis** from the Coursebook.

In this challenge task, you will choose an idea, and then turn it into a question that can be tested by a scientific experiment. Then you will write a plan for the experiment.

Here are two ideas about water plants and photosynthesis.

Idea 1: Carbon dioxide is one of the raw materials for photosynthesis. We can provide extra carbon dioxide to a water plant by bubbling carbon dioxide gas into the water. This could allow the water plant to photosynthesise faster.

Idea 2: Water plants release bubbles of oxygen into the water when they photosynthesise. They need energy for photosynthesis, which they obtain from light. Different colours of light provide different amounts of energy, which affects the rate of photosynthesis.

1 Choose **one** of the ideas. Use the idea to write down a question or **hypothesis** that you could test by doing an experiment.

> Check your question or hypothesis with your teacher before you move on to question 2.

....

....

....

....

2 Use the next two pages to write a plan for an experiment you could do, to answer your question or test your hypothesis.

Try to make your plan really clear and detailed, so that someone else could follow it to do your experiment.

Include a labelled diagram of the apparatus you would use.

Draw a results chart.

Predict what you think the results might be, giving a reason for your prediction.

> Remember to state your independent variable, dependent variable, and the variables that you will try to keep the same.

1 Plants

....
....
....
....
....
....
....
....
....
....
....
....
....
....
....

1.2 Interpreting data about water uptake

This challenge task relates to **1.5 Transporting water and minerals** from the Coursebook.

> In this challenge task, you will look at some data collected by researchers who did experiments on wheat plants. You will choose a good way to display the data, and then use the data to make a suggestion.

A team of scientists wanted to compare how much water is taken up by three different varieties of wheat growing in a cold place.

- They grew seedlings of each of the three varieties of wheat.
- They provided all of the seedlings with the same volume of water.
- They placed the seedlings at a temperature of $2\,°C$.
- They measured how much water each group of seedlings had taken up after two weeks, and again after six weeks.

The table shows the results.

Variety of wheat	Volume of water taken up per g of wheat plant, in cm^3		
	after 2 weeks at $2\,°C$	after 6 weeks at $2\,°C$	
A	78	102	
B	64	94	
C	72	122	

1 Suggest why the scientists measured the volume of water taken up per gram of the wheat plants, rather than the volume taken up by a whole plant.

....

....

....

2 Think about different ways in which you could display these results.

Choose **one** good way, and display the results on the grid on the next page.

3 Compare the volumes of water taken up by the three varieties of wheat after two weeks.

....

....

4 Describe how the results after six weeks are different from those after two weeks.

....

....

5 Plants need to take up water so that they can photosynthesise and grow well.

Suggest which variety of wheat would be the best choice for a farmer in Canada, where the temperatures often fall very low.

Explain your choice.

....

....

....

2.1 Investigating how sugar concentration affects the rate of absorption

This challenge task relates to **2.3 Digestion and absorption** from the Coursebook.

> In this challenge task, you will record the results of an experiment. Then you will write a conclusion and suggest an explanation.

Nor and Elsa did an experiment to find out how the concentration of sugar in a solution affects how quickly it is absorbed through Visking tubing.

Here is the apparatus they used.

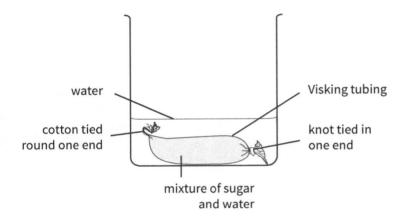

The girls set up three sets of apparatus. They used a different concentration of sugar in each one. The concentrations were 0%, 2% and 4%.

Every five minutes, the girls took samples of the water from each beaker.

They tested each sample for sugar.

Here are their results.

After 5 minutes: 0% blue, 2% blue, 4% green

After 10 minutes: 0% blue, 2% green, 4% brick-red

After 15 minutes: 0% blue, 2% brick-red, 4% brick-red

Which part of the digestive system does the Visking tubing represent?

1 Answer Elsa's question.

....

2 Describe how the girls could test the samples for sugar.

....

....

....

3 Construct a results table below, and fill in the girls' results.

4 Explain why all of the results for the 0% sugar solution were blue.

....

....

....

....

5 Write a **conclusion** for the girls' experiment.

....

....

....

6 Suggest why the apparatus containing the 4% sugar solution produced a brick-red colour sooner than the apparatus containing the 2% sugar solution.

> This is a difficult question! Think about what the particles of sugar in the solution are doing, and how they get out of the Visking tubing.

....

....

....

....

....

....

....

2.2 Investigating the effect of amylase on starch

This challenge task relates to **2.6 Enzymes** from the Coursebook.

> In this challenge task, you will look at the method and results of an enzyme experiment. You will analyse and explain the results, then suggest how the experiment could be modified.

Jon and Sam wanted to find out how temperature affects the rate at which amylase digests starch.

- They put equal volumes of starch solution and amylase solution into 15 test tubes.

- They divided the tubes into five sets of three.

- They stood each set of three test tubes in a water bath at a different temperature. The temperatures were 0 °C, 20 °C, 40 °C, 60 °C and 80 °C.

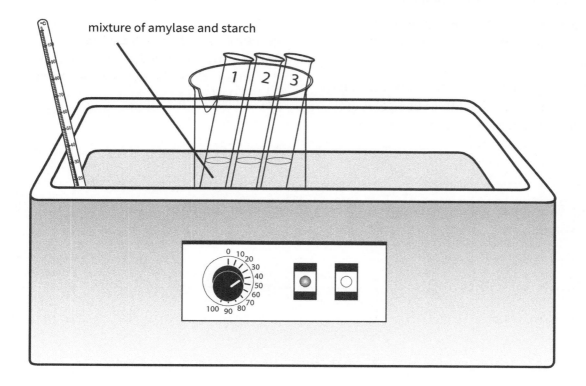
mixture of amylase and starch

Jon used a pipette to take a small sample from each tube every two minutes, and added it to a drop of iodine on a tile.

Sam did the timing. He recorded the first time at which a drop of iodine stayed brown and did **not** turn black when the sample was added.

The table shows their results.

Temperature in °C	Time for iodine test to stay brown in minutes			
	Tube 1	Tube 2	Tube 3	Mean
0	always blue-black	always blue-black	always blue-black	
20	6	4	6	
40	2	2	2	
60	4	10	6	
80	always blue-black	always blue-black	always blue-black	

1 One of the results is **anomalous**. Draw a circle around this result in the table.

2 Calculate the mean for the results at 20 °C, 40 °C and 60 °C. Write your answers in the table.

> Remember **not** to include the anomalous result when you calculate the mean. Write the mean times to one decimal place.

3 When a sample from a test tube gives a blue-black colour when added to iodine solution, what can we conclude about the sample?

....

....

4 Explain why some of the samples gave a brown colour when added to iodine solution.

....

....

....

....

5 The boys decided that their results showed that amylase works fastest
at a temperature of about 40 °C.

Their teacher set them a challenge to find the exact temperature at which
amylase works fastest.

Suggest how the boys could do this. Explain your answer.

....

....

....

....

....

....

....

....

....

3.1 Comparing human and fish circulatory systems

This challenge task relates to **3.1 The human circulatory system** and **3.2 The heart** from the Coursebook.

> In this challenge task, you will read information about the circulatory system of a fish. You will then use the information, and your knowledge of the human circulatory system, to answer questions.

A fish has a heart with only two chambers – an upper chamber and a lower chamber. The blood is pumped out of the lower chamber to the gills, where it picks up oxygen. The blood then flows directly from the gills to the rest of the body. From there, it flows back to the upper chamber of the heart, and then to the lower chamber.

1 Use the information above to sketch a simple plan of a fish's circulatory system.

Label your plan, and include arrows to show the direction of blood flow.

2 Describe how the structure of the heart of a fish differs from the structure of a human heart.

....

....

....

....

3 Name the organs in which blood picks up oxygen:

a in a human ....

b in a fish ....

4 Does the heart of a fish contain oxygenated blood or deoxygenated blood? Explain your answer.

....

....

....

....

5 Describe the main difference between the circulatory system of a fish and the circulatory system of a human.

....

....

....

....

....

3.2 Rats at altitude

This challenge task relates to **3.3 Blood** from the Coursebook.

> In this challenge task, you will use information to make a prediction. You will draw a graph to display a set of results, and think about the design of an experiment.

Our red blood cells carry oxygen around the body. At high altitudes, there is less oxygen in the air.

A team of scientists did an experiment to find out how the number of red blood cells in rats changed when the rats were taken to high altitude.

1 Make a **prediction** about what might happen to the number of red blood cells when the rats were taken to high altitude.

Explain your prediction.

....

....

....

....

This is what the scientists did:

- They kept one group of rats at sea level, and took another group to high altitude.
- They took blood samples from each rat on days 1, 3, 7, 15 and 20.
- They measured the number of red blood cells in a certain volume of blood from each rat. This is called the red blood cell count.
- They calculated the mean red blood cell counts for each group of rats.

Their results are shown in the table.

Time in days	Mean red blood cell count	
	Rats at sea level	**Rats at high altitude**
1	6.5	6.5
3	7.0	8.5
7	6.5	10.0
15	6.5	10.5
20	7.0	11.5

2 On the grid, construct line graphs to show these results. Draw two lines on the same pair of axes.

> Take care with the scale on the *x*-axis.

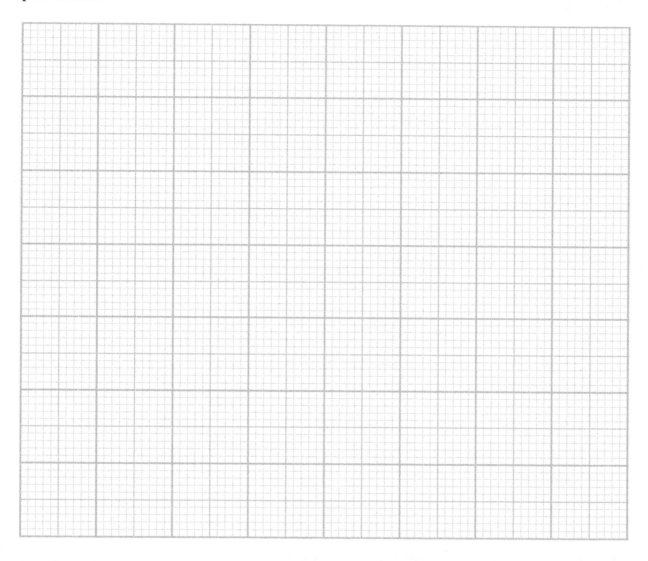

3 What was the **independent** variable in the experiment?

....

4 What was the **dependent** variable in the experiment?

....

5 Suggest **two** variables that the scientists should have kept the same.

....

....

6 Calculate the increase in mean red blood cell count for the rats at high altitude between day 1 and day 20.

Show your working.

....

7 Use your answer to question 6 to calculate the **mean rate of increase per day**.

Show your working.

....

8 After 20 days, the rats at high altitude were taken back down to sea level.

Predict what would happen to their red blood cell count over the next few weeks.

Explain your answer.

....

....

....

....

4.1 Lung volume at different ages

This challenge task relates to **4.1 The human respiratory system** from the Coursebook.

> In this challenge task, you will practise finding information on a graph. You will do a simple calculation, and use evidence from the graph to make some predictions.

Several hundred men and women of different ages had their lung volumes investigated. They were asked to push out as much air as they could in one breath.

The mean values of volume of air pushed out for each age group were then calculated.

The graph shows the results.

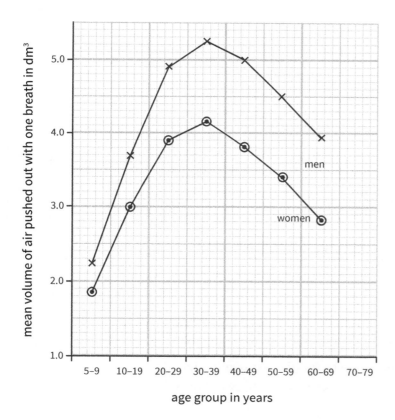

1 Suggest why the researchers collected results from several hundred men and women, rather than just a few in each age group.

....

....

....

2 State the mean volume of air pushed out for women in the 20 to 29 age group.

....

Remember to include the unit in your answer.

3 Calculate the difference between the mean volumes of air pushed out for men and women in the 40 to 49 age group.

Show your working.

....

4 Describe how the mean volume of air that can be pushed out by women changes with age.

....

....

....

5 Use the graph to predict a value for the mean volume of air that can be pushed out by men aged between 70 and 79.

....

6 The people sampled were all non-smokers. People who smoke cigarettes can usually push out less air in one breath than people who do not smoke.

On the graph on the previous page, draw a line to predict the results that might be obtained if female smokers from the ages of 20 to 69 were tested.

4.2 Looking at data on giving up smoking

This challenge task relates to **4.5 Cigarettes and health** from the Coursebook.

In this challenge task, you will practise finding information in text. You will select some of this information to construct a results chart and draw a graph. Lastly, you will combine information from different sources to make a suggestion.

In 2003, a survey was carried out in China to investigate how many smokers had given up smoking, or wanted to give up smoking.

The survey found that 2.5% of men and 3.2% of women had successfully given up smoking. Another 3.6% of men and 3.9% of women were trying to give up smoking.

The people who had been successful in giving up smoking were asked why they had given up. 41% said that it was because they had got ill, and 27% said that it was because they were worried that they might get ill. 12% had given up because of the cost of cigarettes. 5% had given up because their families disapproved of them smoking, and another 5% because their doctor had told them to. The remainder had a mixture of different reasons for giving up.

The survey also collected data about people who had tried to give up smoking, but had failed. 54% of these people said they had gone back to smoking because they couldn't manage without cigarettes. 4% said their health had improved, so they thought it would be OK to start smoking again. 30% explained that it was difficult not to smoke when everyone else around them was smoking. The remaining 12% had other reasons for failing to give up smoking.

1   When you have read the whole text carefully, choose **one** set of the survey results that you can use to construct a results table and graph.

Write down what your chosen set of results is about.

....

....

2 Construct a results table, and fill in your chosen results.

3 Display your data in the best way you can. For example, you could use a pie chart in the space below or a bar graph on the grid opposite.

4 Since the survey was carried out, electronic cigarettes (e-cigarettes) have become available. These provide the smoker with nicotine, but are less likely to make the smoker ill.

Using the information from the survey, and your knowledge of the effects of nicotine, suggest how e-cigarettes might help more people to give up smoking.

> You may need to read the text again.
>
> If you need a reminder of the effects of nicotine, look in your Coursebook section 4.5.

....

....

....

....

5.1 Growth of girls and boys in India

This challenge task relates to **5.5 Growth and development** from the Coursebook.

> In this challenge task, you will use a graph to calculate growth rate.
> You will then use extra information to add a second curve to the graph.

The graph shows the mean height of girls in India at different ages.

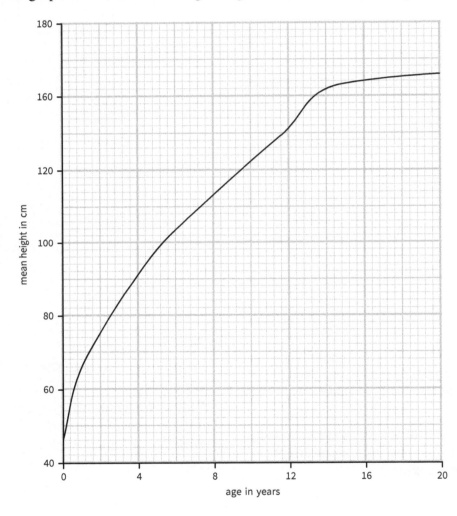

1 State the mean height of girls in India at birth.

....

2 State the mean height of girls in India at 12 years old.

....

> Remember to include the unit in your answer.

3 Calculate the change in mean height between birth and 12 years old.

....

4 Use your answer to question 3 to calculate the mean rate of growth, in cm per year, between birth and 12 years old.

....

5 A steeply rising line on the graph shows a fast rate of growth.

Between which ages do girls in India grow most rapidly?

....

6 The mean heights of boys and girls in India are similar until they are about 14 years old. After that, most boys grow faster than girls, reaching a mean height of about 175 cm by the time they are 20 years old.

Use this information to sketch a line on the graph opposite to show the mean height of boys in India from birth to age 20.

5.2 Using apps and smart watches to monitor lifestyle

This challenge task relates to **5.6 Lifestyle and health** from the Coursebook.

> In this challenge task, you will use your scientific understanding of how lifestyle affects health to write about the possible effects of personal data-tracking apps.

Many people use a phone app or smart watch to track information about what they do each day.

For example, they monitor how much exercise they do, what they eat, or how well they sleep.

> 'Monitor' means to measure and record over a period of time or at regular intervals.

1 Write three or more paragraphs to discuss whether you think apps and smart watches can help people to lead a healthy lifestyle.

Make sure that your discussion includes:

- facts about how lifestyle affects health

- information about what personal data can be recorded using phone apps or smart watches

- your ideas, based on scientific understanding, about whether these devices can help a person to stay healthy.

> You can do internet research about the use of these devices. Take care to choose websites that provide you with reliable information. Remember that people trying to sell a product may exaggerate how useful their product is.

....

....

....

....

....

....

6.1 Comparing the diffusion of two dyes

This challenge task relates to **6.3 Investigating diffusion** from the Coursebook.

> In this challenge task, you will discuss an investigation and present results.

Sam is asked to carry out an investigation to compare how quickly two different food dyes diffuse in water at different temperatures.

He carries out the same test with a blue dye and then a red dye.

1 In the test with each dye, what is

    a the **independent** variable? ....

    b the **dependent** variable? ....

2 Which variables must Sam keep the same when he tests both dyes, so that he can compare the results?

....

....

....

3 The table below and the table on the next page show Sam's results.

Present these results on the graph grid on the next page.

Join the plotted points appropriately.

> First calculate the mean times. Write the mean times to one decimal place.
>
> Ignore any anomalous results when calculating the means.

Results for the blue dye

Temperature in °C	Time taken for dye to diffuse completely in s			
	First attempt	Second attempt	Third attempt	Mean
20	108	100	103	
30	75	69	73	
40	49	55	53	
50	39	39	45	
60	26	34	30	
70	18	24	19	

Results for the red dye

Temperature in °C	Time taken for dye to diffuse completely in s			
	First attempt	Second attempt	Third attempt	Mean
20	50	53	56	
30	42	44	48	
40	35	34	30	
50	25	41	27	
60	21	19	20	
70	20	18	22	

4 Describe what the results for the blue dye tell you.

....

....

....

....

5 Describe what the results for the red dye tell you.

....

....

....

....

6 Compare the results for the two dyes.

....

....

....

....

....

....

6.2 Explaining Brownian motion

This challenge task relates to **6.4 Brownian motion** from the Coursebook.

> In this challenge task, you will predict and explain observations using your scientific knowledge and understanding.

Thousands of years ago, the Greeks thought that all substances were made up of small particles, but they could not prove it.

In the early 19th century, a biologist called Robert Brown examined some pollen grains in water using a microscope. He noticed that the pollen grains were constantly moving in a random way. This type of motion is now called Brownian motion.

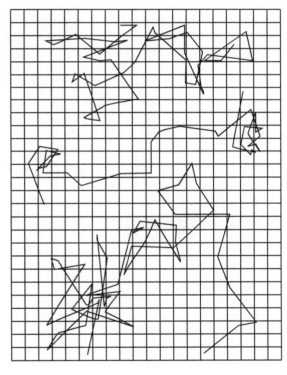

These are Robert Brown's drawings of the motion of three pollen grains, as he watched them through the microscope.

Robert Brown could not explain why the pollen grains moved in this way. He thought that the pollen grains might be moving actively – 'swimming' – in the water. He tested his idea by looking at some dust in water through the microscope. The dust moved in the same way.

He still could not explain the motion.

Brownian motion can be explained using particle theory. The particles of the water are themselves moving about. The very small water particles constantly collide with the pollen or dust particles and cause them to move around. The water particles are far too small to see, even with a microscope.

1 Why could the Greeks not prove that all matter is made of very small particles?

....

....

2 What was Robert Brown's first idea about why the pollen grains moved?

....

....

3 How did he find out that this first idea was wrong?

....

....

....

....

4 Explain why the pollen grains moved about randomly and not in any one direction.

....

....

....

....

....

5 If Robert Brown had observed pollen grains in warmer water, suggest his observations. Explain your answer.

....

....

....

6 Imagine millions of pollen grains mixed with a single drop of water. Suggest what you would observe, and explain your answer.

....

....

....

....

6.3 Pressure in bottled gas

This challenge task relates to **6.5 Gas pressure** from the Coursebook.

> In this challenge task, you will explain gas pressure in terms of particles.

If you take a plastic bag and hold it open in the air, the air in the bag and the air in the room are at the same pressure.

If you hold the bag closed and squeeze the air in it into a smaller and smaller space, the pressure of the air in the bag is higher.

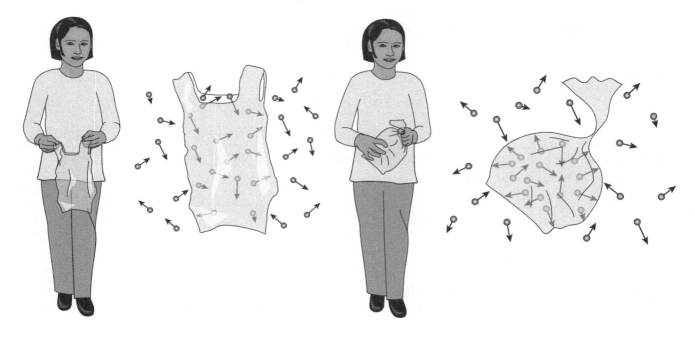

1 What causes the increase in gas pressure when the bag is squeezed?

  ....

  ....

  ....

2 What will happen if someone makes a hole in the bag that Anna is squeezing?
  Explain your answer.

  ....

  ....

Gas used for cooking is sold in metal bottles. The gas is forced into a small space to make it easier to transport.

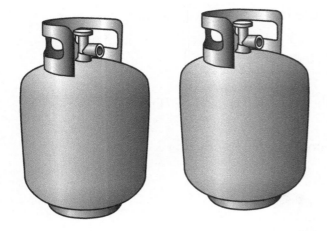

3 Suggest why cooking-gas bottles are made with thick strong walls.

....

....

4 If you shake a bottle of cooking gas, you can hear a liquid moving about. Suggest an explanation for this.

....

....

....

5 Gas bottles are very dangerous in a fire.
Explain what happens to the particles inside the bottle as the temperature rises.

....

....

6 Describe what will happen if the temperature continues to rise.

....

....

....

....

Unit 7 Elements and compounds

7.1 Elements in the Moon's crust

This challenge task relates to **7.2 Atoms and elements** from the Coursebook.

> In this challenge task, you will practise presenting information as a pie chart.

The table gives details of the most abundant (common) elements in rocks on the Moon's surface.

Element	Percentage of Moon's crust
oxygen	43%
silicon	20%
magnesium	19%
iron	10%
aluminium	3%
calcium	3%
other elements	2%

1 Present this information as a pie chart in the space below.

> You will need a protractor and a pair of compasses to complete this task.

7.2 Building the Periodic Table

This challenge task relates to **7.3 The Periodic Table** from the Coursebook.

> In this challenge task, you will see how advances in scientific understanding are made, by scientists developing the ideas of others and using creative thinking.

Scientists often try to make sense of large amounts of information by grouping similar things together. For example, they group similar types of animals together – mammals, fish, insects, and so on.

It was the same for elements, as more and more were discovered.

Three important scientists contributed to the Periodic Table that we use today. The timeline and information below explain their ideas and work.

—— 1817 ———————— 1864 ———————— 1869 ——

Johann Dobereiner	**John Newlands**	**Dmitri Mendeleev**
'Law of Triads'	every eighth element had similar properties	modified and extended John Newlands' work

In **1817**, a scientist called Johann Dobereiner put forward his **'Law of Triads'**. He grouped similar elements together in threes, based on their appearance and properties.

Around the same time, scientists began to find out the mass of the atoms of the elements.

The table on the right shows one of Dobereiner's triads. The numbers are the atomic masses of the elements.

In **1864**, John Newlands arranged the 63 known elements in order of the mass of their atoms. He started with the lightest. He noticed that every eighth element in his arrangement had similar properties – a similar element appeared **periodically**.

But this pattern, of similar elements appearing every eighth time, did not continue through all the elements.

In **1869**, a schoolteacher, Dmitri Mendeleev, **used John Newlands' ideas**. He left gaps in the arrangement of elements so that the pattern of eights continued. He also swapped the position of some elements, so that elements with similar properties were always grouped together.

Mendeleev predicted the properties of some undiscovered elements that would fill the gaps in his 'periodic table'. His predictions turned out to be correct. Mendeleev's table forms the basis of the Periodic Table we use today.

> 'Triad' is a name for a group of three related things.

Salt-forming elements	
lithium	3
sodium	23
potassium	39

> Scientists learn from one another and this helps them to develop ideas.

The first 20 elements in the Periodic Table

								H hydrogen										He helium
Li lithium	Be beryllium											B boron	C carbon	N nitrogen	O oxygen	F fluorine		Ne neon
Na sodium	Mg magnesium											Al aluminium	Si silicon	P phosphorus	S sulfur	Cl chlorine		Ar argon
K potassium	Ca calcium																	

1 How did Johann Dobereiner arrange the elements?

....

....

2 Suggest how Dobereiner's ideas influenced John Newlands' ideas.

....

....

3 Why did the pattern in Newlands' table not continue?

....

....

4 Describe how Dmitri Mendeleev modified Newlands' table.

....

....

....

5 Mendeleev's table did not contain helium, argon or neon. Suggest why.

....

6 Look at the diagram of the Periodic Table above. Which element
would you expect to have similar properties to chlorine? ....

7 How many elements are known today? ....

8 Name **at least two** elements that are made by scientists.
These are sometimes called 'synthetic' elements.

> To complete questions
> 7 and 8 you will need
> to do some research.

....

....

....

7.3 Formula quiz

This challenge task relates to **7.5 Formulae** from the Coursebook.

In this challenge task, you will write and understand formulae of common compounds.

Check your knowledge of compound formulae.

1 The formulae for the common acids used in school laboratories are
   HCl, H_2SO_4 and HNO_3.

   Write down the following information for each of these.

   HCl

   Name of acid ....

   Number of atoms of each element in this molecule

   ....

   H₂SO₄

   Name of acid ....

   Number of atoms of each element in this molecule

   ....

   ....

   HNO₃

   Name of acid ....

   Number of atoms of each element in this molecule

   ....

   ....

2 There is one element that **all** acids contain. Name this element.

....

3 The following formulae are written incorrectly. Rewrite them correctly.

a NA_2CO_3 ....

b $CaCl2$ ....

c $CaCO^3$ ....

d $O2$ ....

e $2Cl$ ....

f K_2Co_3 ....

4 The formula for the sugar molecule called maltose is $C_{12}H_{22}O_{11}$.
What does this tell you about what the molecule is made of?

....

....

5 What does $2C_{12}H_{22}O_{11}$ mean?

....

6 a $Mg(OH)_2$ is the formula for which compound?

....

b How many oxygen atoms are in this molecule? ....

c How many hydrogen atoms are in this molecule? ....

7 Write the name and the formula for a compound of calcium that contains oxygen and hydrogen atoms.

....

....

8.1 A frozen mixture of salt and water

This challenge task relates to **8.2 More about mixtures** from the Coursebook.

> In this challenge task, you will identify variables and plot a graph with negative numbers.

The melting point of ice changes if the salinity (saltiness) of the ice is changed. Some scientists are investigating this effect.

They dissolve a measured mass of salt in water. They freeze the mixture at a temperature of −15 °C.

They then crush the ice and place it in a filter funnel.

The ice drips when it starts to melt. The temperature is measured; this is the melting point.

The scientists repeat the procedure using ice of different salinities.

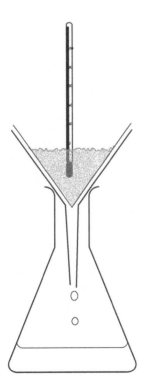

1 When preparing the frozen samples, the mass of salt added is changed.

What must be kept the same?

....

The table shows the scientists' results.

Mass of salt dissolved in g	Melting point in °C
0	0
1	−2
2	−4
3	−5.5
4	−2.5
5	−10
6	−12.5

2 Plot the results on the graph grid.

Most of the temperatures are lower than zero. Think about how you will arrange the temperature scale.

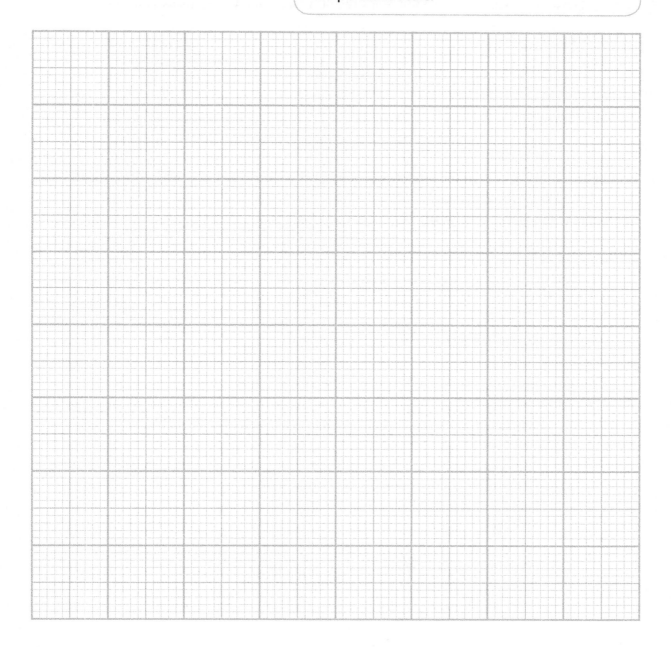

3 One of the results does not fit the pattern. Ring this plotted point on your graph.

4 Draw a **line of best fit**.

5 What **conclusion** can you make from these results?

....

....

6 Suggest possible reasons for the anomalous result. List as many reasons as you can.

....

....

....

....

....

7 In countries that are cold in the winter, salt is often spread on the roads when the temperature starts to fall below freezing.

Explain how this helps to keep the roads safer.

....

....

....

....

....

....

8.2 Extracting salt

This challenge task relates to **8.5 Solutions** from the Coursebook.

> In this challenge task, you will read some information about how salt is extracted. Then you will answer some questions and explain why the salt extraction is done in this way.

Sodium chloride, also known as common salt, is a very useful compound. Read this information about how it is extracted.

In hot countries, salt is extracted directly from seawater. Seawater is mainly a mixture of water and sodium chloride. In order to extract the salt, seawater is trapped in large shallow pools. The heat energy from the Sun evaporates the water to leave the salt behind.

In some countries, salt is found underground as rock salt. Rock salt is a mixture of sodium chloride and rock, such as sandstone. To mine the rock salt, shafts are drilled down into the rock. In the mine, cutters and explosives are then used to extract the rock salt. This is brought to the surface, where it is crushed. This form of salt is used on the roads in cold countries in the winter. The rock salt needs to be treated to extract the pure salt if it is to be used for chemical reactions or for food.

Some rock salt is extracted by a different method of mining, called solution mining. Water is pumped down a well drilled into the rock salt. The salt dissolves in the water and this is pumped back to the surface. The water is then evaporated to leave behind the salt.

Now answer the questions on the next page.

1 What is the solvent in seawater? ....

2 What is the main solute in seawater? ....

3 Explain why the seawater is trapped in large shallow pools and not in small deep ones.

....

....

....

4 Suggest why this method is not used in colder countries.

....

....

5 Describe the dangers in mining rock salt.

....

....

....

....

6 What further advantage does solution mining have compared with rock salt mining?

....

....

7 Suggest how rock salt can be purified, so that the salt is clean and free from rock fragments.

....

....

....

....

8.3 Comparing the solubility of two salts

This challenge task relates to **8.7 Solubility investigation** from the Coursebook.

In this challenge task, you will plan an investigation and interpret some results.

Amal and Jon are asked to compare the solubility of two salts in water at room temperature. The two salts are labelled X and Y.

1 Name the **independent** variable in the investigation.

....

2 Name the **dependent** variable in the investigation.

....

3 List the **control** variables in the investigation.

....

....

4 Describe how Amal and Jon will carry out this investigation. They have access to normal laboratory equipment. You may draw diagrams if this helps your description.

....

....

....

....

....

....

Amal and Jon carry out the experiment and find that more of salt X than salt Y can be dissolved in water at room temperature.

The boys then investigate the solubility of these two salts at different temperatures.

The graph shows the results of their investigation.

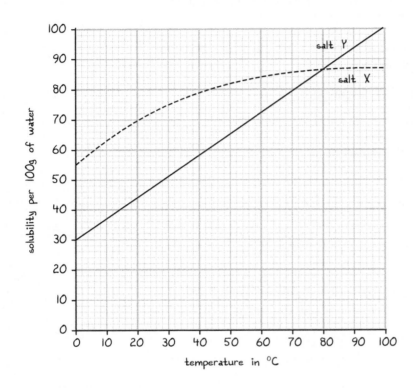

5 At what temperature do the two salts have the same solubility? ....

6 Which salt is the **least** soluble at 50 °C? ....

7 Describe what the graph shows about the solubility of salt X.

....

....

....

....

8 Describe what the graph shows about the solubility of salt Y.

....

....

....

....

9.1 Writing word equations

This challenge task relates to **9.3 Reactions with acids** from the Coursebook.

> In this challenge task, you will write word equations and identify the elements contained in a product that is a compound.

1 Write the word equation for the reaction between zinc and nitric acid.

2 An acid is added to a carbonate to make calcium chloride. Write the word equation for this reaction.

3 In a reaction between a compound and an acid, a gas is given off. This gas turns limewater milky. What information does this give you about the compound?

....

4 Write the word equation for the reaction between zinc and sulfuric acid.

5 The gas given off in the reaction in question 4 burns in air with a squeaky pop.

Write the word equation for the reaction of this gas with oxygen.

6 Which elements are present in sulfuric acid?

....

7 Which elements are present in copper carbonate?

....

9.2 Is more gas produced when more metal is used?

This challenge task relates to **9.3 Reactions with acids** from the Coursebook.

> In this challenge task, you will plot a graph of some data from a metal/acid reaction, and interpret the results.

Nor and Elsa reacted a metal with an acid. They used the apparatus shown below to measure the volume of gas given off when acid was added to the metal. They measured the volume of the gas **only** when all the metal had disappeared.

The girls investigated how changing the mass of metal used would change the volume of gas produced.

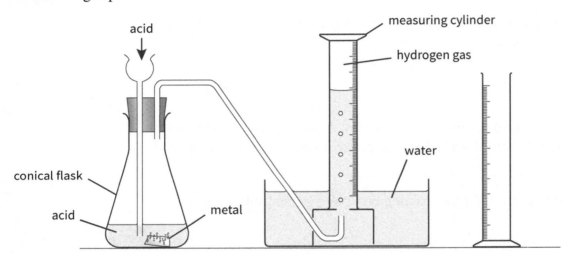

These are their results.

Mass of metal that reacted in g	Volume of hydrogen given off in cm³
0.5	700
1.0	1200
1.5	1500
2.0	2200
2.5	2600
3.0	3100
3.5	3500
4.0	4100
4.5	4500
5.0	5100

1 Plot the data on the graph grid on the next page and draw a line of best fit.

2 State conclusions you can make from the results.

....

....

3 If you did this experiment but only had measuring cylinders that hold 500 cm³,
what problem would you have in getting accurate results?

....

....

4 The reactants used in this investigation were zinc and sulfuric acid.
What were the products?

....

5 If magnesium and hydrochloric acid were used, what would the products be?

....

9.3 Investigating burning magnesium

This challenge task relates to **9.5 More about conservation of mass** from the Coursebook.

> In this challenge task, you will make a conclusion from experimental data and consider the practical problems of carrying out an investigation.

In an investigation, magnesium is burned in a **limited** volume of pure oxygen. The aim of the investigation is to answer this question:

How does the mass of the compound formed depend on the mass of magnesium burned?

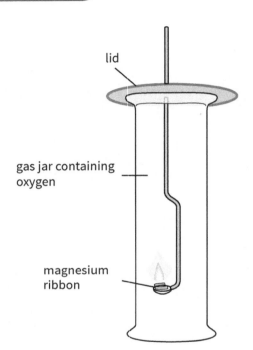

1 What variables need to be **controlled** to make this investigation fair?

   ....

   ....

   ....

   ....

2 Write the word equation for the reaction between magnesium and oxygen.

These results are obtained.

Mass of magnesium burned in g	Mass of compound formed in g
0.5	0.9
1.0	1.8
1.5	2.6
2.0	3.4
2.5	3.4
3.0	3.4

3 Plot the results on the grid opposite. Join the points appropriately.

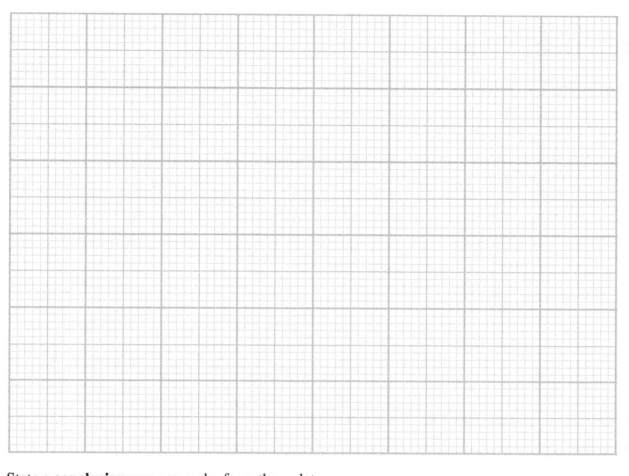

4 State a **conclusion** you can make from these data.

....

....

5 Explain why the mass of compound formed stays the same when the mass
of magnesium used increases from 2.0 g to 3.0 g.

....

....

6 If you carried out this investigation in the laboratory, suggest:

a problems you could have in getting **accurate** results

....

....

b safety aspects you should consider.

....

....

10.1 Units of speed

This challenge task relates to **10.1 How fast? – Measuring speed** and **10.3 Speed calculations** from the Coursebook.

In this challenge task, you will do some calculations about speed and convert between units of speed.

Speed is often measured in units of m/s (metres per second) or km/h (kilometres per hour).

1 Calculate the number of seconds in **one hour**.

Show your working.

.... s

2 How many metres are there in **one kilometre**? .... m

3 A car is travelling at 50 km/h.

How many **metres** does it travel in **one hour**?

Show your working.

.... m

4 Use your answer from question 3 to calculate how many **metres** the car travels in **one second**.

Show your working. Give your answer to the nearest whole number.

.... m/s

5 For each of these calculations, show your working.

a A horse runs at 36 km/h. **Convert** this speed into m/s.

Give your answer to the nearest whole number.

> The method in questions 3 and 4 can be used to convert km/h into m/s.

.... m/s

b A racing motorcycle goes at 300 km/h. Convert this speed into m/s.

Give your answer to the nearest whole number.

.... m/s

c Amal walks at an average speed of 5 km/h. What is his average speed in m/s?

Give your answer to one decimal place.

.... m/s

10.2 Measuring speed

This challenge task relates to **10.2 Speed check** and **10.3 Speed calculations** from the Coursebook.

> In this challenge task, you will consider how speed cameras work.

Two different systems are used to check the speed of cars.

System A detects the speed of a car.

If the speed is too high, a camera takes two photographs.

The photographs are taken with a time interval of 0.5 s.

There are white lines on the road 1 m apart to show how far the car travelled in the 0.5 s time interval.

1 Calculate how many metres a car will travel between the two photographs when it is travelling at 40 km/h.

Show your working.

Give your answer to one decimal place.

.... m

> If you need a reminder of the formulae for calculating distance, speed or time, look in your Coursebook section 10.3.

System B is another type of speed-check system that photographs a car as it crosses a white line.

A second camera photographs the car as it crosses another white line 1 km further along the road.

The time between the two photographs is used to calculate the speed.

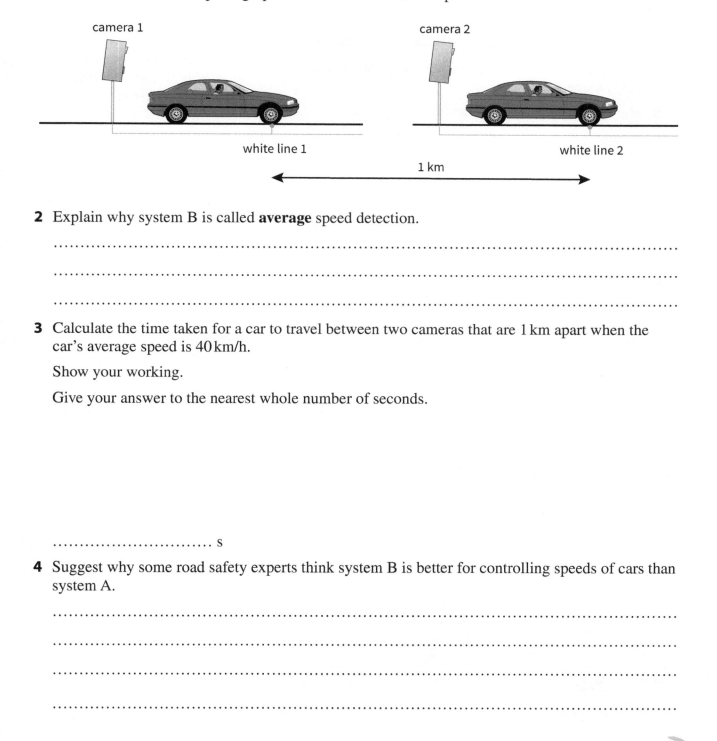

2 Explain why system B is called **average** speed detection.

....

....

....

3 Calculate the time taken for a car to travel between two cameras that are 1 km apart when the car's average speed is 40 km/h.

Show your working.

Give your answer to the nearest whole number of seconds.

.... s

4 Suggest why some road safety experts think system B is better for controlling speeds of cars than system A.

....

....

....

....

10.3 Showing speed in graphs

This challenge task relates to **10.5 Distance/time graphs** from the Coursebook.

> In this challenge task, you will draw some distance/time graphs.

1 Use the axes provided to sketch **distance/time graphs** for:

A an object that is moving at a constant speed and then stops moving

B an object that is moving at an increasing speed

C an object that is moving at a fast constant speed then moves at a slower constant speed.

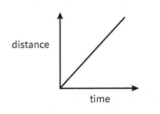

This distance/time graph represents an object moving at a **constant speed**.

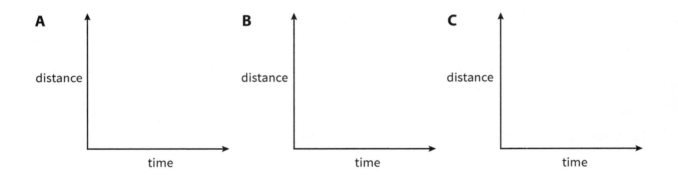

A distance / time

B distance / time

C distance / time

Elsa and Nor are together on a road.

Elsa starts to walk.

She starts walking at time = 0 seconds.

She walks at a constant speed of 2 m/s.

2 Draw a line on the grid to represent Elsa walking. Label your line E.

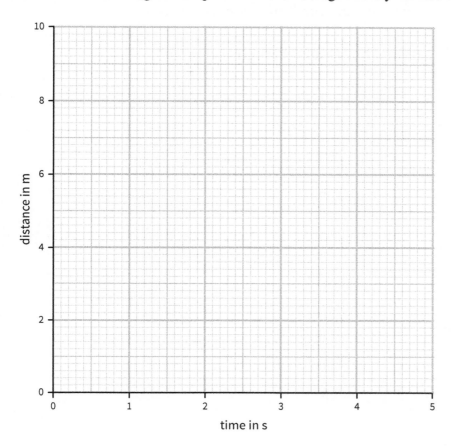

Nor starts to cycle after Elsa.

Nor starts cycling at time = 2 seconds.

Nor cycles with a constant speed of 4 m/s.

3 Draw another line on the grid above to represent Nor cycling. Label your line N.

4 Use the graph to work out at what time Nor passes Elsa.

Show on the graph how you worked out your answer.

5 Use the graph to work out the distance that they have travelled when Nor passes Elsa.

Show on the graph how you worked out your answer.

Jon walks along a path which has a total length of 50 m. He starts at one end of the path.

For the first 10 s he walks at 2 m/s.

He then stops for 20 s.

He then walks to the end of the path at a constant speed. He arrives at the end of the path 60 s after he started.

6 Draw a distance/time graph to represent Jon's walk on the grid below.

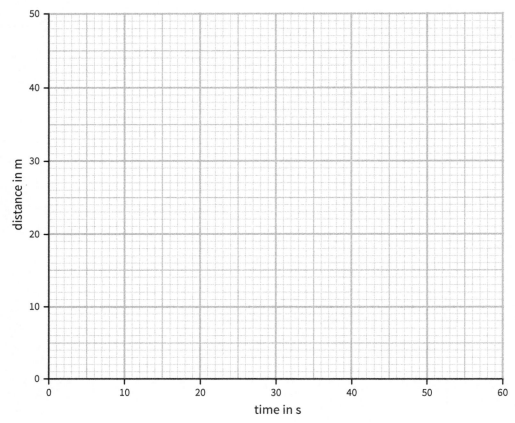

7 What was Jon's walking speed for the last part of his journey?

.... m/s

Unit 11 Sound

11.1 Sound measurements

This challenge task relates to **11.3 How sound travels** from the Coursebook.

> In this challenge task, you will do some calculations about sound travelling, and consider how sound travels.

Jon is watching a firework display.

1 Jon always sees the fireworks explode **before** he hears the sound they make.

Explain why.

....

....

....

2 Jon uses a stopwatch to measure the time between seeing a firework and hearing it. He does this five times.

All five fireworks are set off from the same place.

Jon does **not** move while making his measurements.

Why is Jon careful not to move while making his measurements?

....

....

....

Jon records his results.

Firework number	Time between seeing and hearing the firework in s
1	1.6
2	1.7
3	1.5
4	2.3
5	1.7

3 Use the results in the table to calculate the **average** time between Jon seeing and hearing a firework.

Do **not** include any anomalous results.

Show your working and give your answer to the same number of significant figures as the results in the table.

Average = ………………………….

4 Use your answer from question 3 to calculate the distance between Jon and the fireworks.

The speed of sound in air is 340 m/s.

Show your working and give your answer to the nearest whole number.

Distance = …………………………

5 Jon sees Amal and calls him over.

When he meets Amal, Jon moves forward by approximately 0.5 m.

Suggest what effect, if any, this would have on any more time measurements that Jon makes.

Explain your answer.

……

……

……

……

6 The particles in air are closer together at sea level than they are at high altitude, such as on tall mountains.

Suggest how the speed of sound in air changes with altitude.
Explain your answer using ideas about how sound travels.

....

....

....

....

7 Whales are large mammals that live in water.

Whales communicate with each other by making sounds.

Two whales are 3500 m apart.

3500 m

One of them makes a sound.

This sound takes 2.36 s to reach the other whale.

Calculate the speed of sound in water.

Show your working and give your answer to the nearest whole number.

Speed of sound in water = ...

8 The speed of sound in air is 340 m/s. Explain why the speed of sound in water is different from the speed of sound in air.

....

....

....

....

11.2 Drawing sound waves

This challenge task relates to **11.4 Sounds on a screen** from the Coursebook.

> In this challenge task, you will draw different sound waves as they would appear on an oscilloscope screen. You will also draw a graph of how the loudness of a sound changes with distance from the sound.

Sam plays a note on his flute. This produces a sound wave in the air.

The sound wave is detected by a microphone and displayed on an oscilloscope screen.

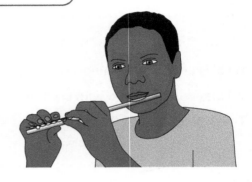

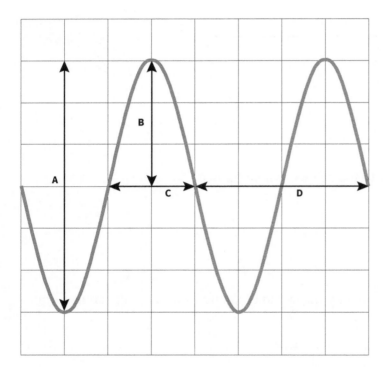

1 Give the letter that represents the **amplitude** of this wave ....

2 Sam plays a different note. The **pitch** is **higher** than the first note. The loudness is the same.

Draw, on the grid below, how this sound would appear on the oscilloscope screen.

Higher pitch

3 Sam now plays the first note again, but more quietly. The pitch is the same as at the start. The **loudness** of the sound is now **decreased**.

Draw, on the grid below, how this sound would appear on the oscilloscope screen.

Decreased loudness

4 Explain why the loudness of a sound decreases as you move further away from the source of the sound.

....

....

....

Elsa uses a microphone and an oscilloscope to measure how the relative loudness of a sound depends on the distance from the sound.

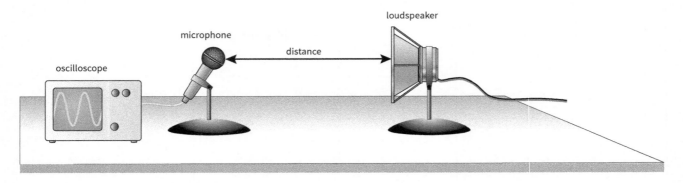

The table shows her results.

Distance in cm	Relative loudness
0	10.00
10	2.50
20	1.25
30	0.62
40	0.40
50	0.28

5 Plot these results as a line graph on the grid on the next page.

Put **relative loudness** on the *y*-axis and **distance** on the *x*-axis.

Draw a **smooth curve** through your points.

6 Describe the pattern shown in the results.

....

....

....

....

7 Explain why relative loudness is on the *y*-axis, and distance is on the *x*-axis for this graph.

....

....

....

8 State **two** variables that Elsa should have kept constant during this investigation.

....

....

Elsa now moves the microphone so it is touching the speaker – at distance 0 cm from the speaker.

She makes the speaker produce the same sound as in her first investigation.

She then moves the microphone away from the speaker slowly, at a **constant speed**.

9 Sketch on the grid how the wave on the oscilloscope screen would change as Elsa moves the microphone.

Moving away at constant speed

12.1 Reflections from mirrors

This challenge task relates to **12.3 How reflections form** from the Coursebook.

> In this challenge task, you will make predictions about light reflecting from a mirror.

Nor is investigating how the angle of reflection of a light ray from a mirror depends on the angle of incidence.

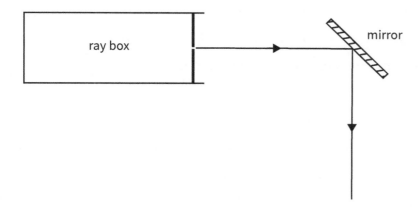

1 On the diagram below, label the angle of incidence with the letter **i** **and** the angle of reflection with the letter **r**.

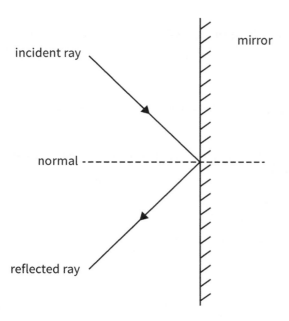

The table shows some of Nor's results.

Angle of incidence in °	Angle of reflection in °
10	10
20	24
30	30
40	40
50	50

2 One of Nor's results has **not** been measured correctly. Which one? ....

3 Explain how you can tell that this result was **not** measured correctly.

....

....

4 When the angle of incidence is 0°, it is **not** possible to see the angle of reflection.

Explain why.

....

....

....

5 Nor sets the angle of incidence to 30°.

Then she turns the mirror by 10° in the direction of the arrows in the diagram.

She does **not** move the ray box that is producing the incident ray.

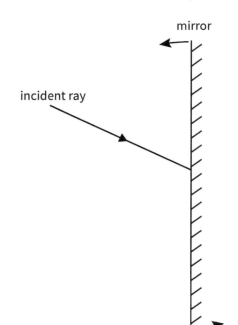

What happens to the angle of incidence as Nor turns the mirror as shown in the diagram?

....

6 As Nor turns the mirror, she observes that the reflected ray also turns.

What angle does the reflected ray turn through as the mirror is turned by 10°?

....

12.2 Refraction by glass and water

This challenge task relates to **12.4 How light bends** from the Coursebook.

> In this challenge task, you will consider how light is refracted by glass and suggest explanations for how things are seen under water.

Jon uses a rectangular glass block to investigate refraction.

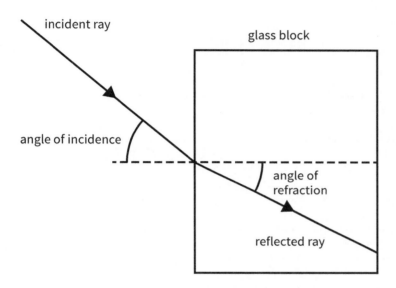

1 On the diagram, draw the light ray that **emerges** from the glass block.

2 Jon puts the glass block on a piece of white paper so he can draw the positions of the light rays.

   Suggest how he can draw the positions of the rays accurately. Remember that during the investigation, the refracted ray is covered by the glass block.

   ....

   ....

   ....

Jon records results and plots the graph shown below.

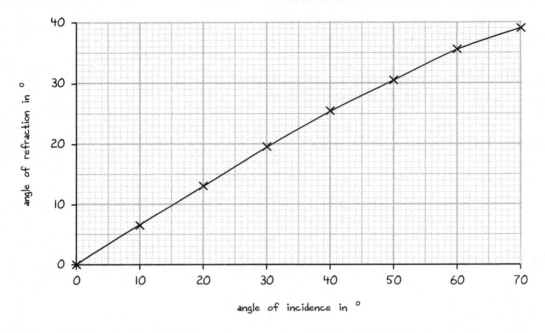

3 Describe the pattern in the results.

....

....

....

....

The heron is a bird that eats fish.

The heron stands in shallow water and waits for fish to swim past. It then catches the fish in its beak.

The diagram shows how the light rays come from the fish to the heron's eye.

The light ray coming to the heron's eye will appear to have come in a **straight line** from the fish.

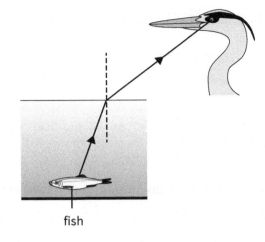

fish

4 The diagram shows the **actual** position of a fish in the water.

On the diagram, write a letter **X** to mark the position of the fish as it **appears** to the heron.

5 The water surface in the diagram is flat.

Explain why it is more difficult for the heron to catch fish when there are waves on the water surface.

....

....

....

Some other birds catch fish by diving into the water from above.

These birds watch the fish from directly above, then dive straight down into the water.

6 Explain why it is easier for these birds to judge the position of the fish, than for the heron.

....

....

....

12.3 Using coloured filters

This challenge task relates to **12.5 The spectrum of white light** and **12.6 Coloured light** from the Coursebook.

In this challenge task, you will predict how light behaves as it passes through coloured filters.

Elsa and Amal are investigating coloured filters.

1 Elsa shines **white light** from a lamp through each filter separately.

Write down the colour of light that comes through the

a red filter ....

b green filter ....

c blue filter ....

d yellow filter ....

2 Amal has a lamp that produces **blue light**.

What will he see when he looks at the lamp

a through a blue filter? ....

b through a red filter? ....

3 Amal now uses the lamp that produces **white light**.

He positions a red filter and a green filter in line with the lamp as shown in the diagram.

lamp producing white light   red filter   green filter

X   Y

What will Amal see when he looks at the lamp

a from position **X** on the diagram? ....

b from position **Y** on the diagram? ....

Elsa darkens the room. She then shines white light from a torch (flashlight) through a green filter. She looks around her room at different objects.

4 Complete the sentences to show what colour each of these objects appears.

   a Her green jacket appears ....

   b A piece of white paper appears ....

   c Her black shoes appear ....

   d A red flower appears ....

Elsa now uses white light from a ray box and a triangular prism to produce a spectrum of light on a screen.

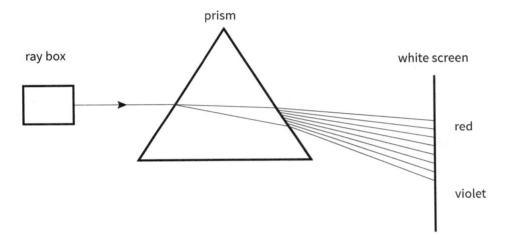

5 Describe what Elsa will see on the screen if she puts

   a a red filter between the ray box and the prism

   ....

   b a red filter between the ray-box and the prism **and** a violet filter between the prism and the screen at the **same time**.

   ....

13.1 Investigating materials

This challenge task relates to **13.1 Magnets and magnetic materials** and **13.2 Magnetic poles** from the Coursebook.

> In this challenge task, you will answer some questions about magnets. Then you will consider the accuracy of experiments and how to select reliable information from research on the internet.

1 Explain the meanings of the terms below.

a magnetic

....

b magnetised

....

Elsa has three metal blocks that look the same.

- One of the metal blocks is made of aluminium.
- One of them is made of iron and has been magnetised.
- One of them is made of iron and has **not** been magnetised.

Elsa does **not** know which is which.

2 Describe how she could use a bar magnet to find out which is which.

....

....

....

....

....

....

Nor is researching magnetic materials on the internet.

She finds three websites:

- website 1, where anyone can post questions and other people can post answers
- website 2, which is written by an educational organisation specially for schools
- website 3, which is written by a university for the university students.

3 Explain the advantages and disadvantages of each of these websites.

Comment on how **reliable** the information is likely to be **and** how useful Nor will find the information.

....

....

....

....

....

....

....

....

....

Jon is comparing the strengths of some bar magnets.

He knows that the magnets are quite similar in strength.

He has two sizes of magnetic paper clips.

large   small

4 State and explain which size of paper clips Jon should use to compare the strengths of the magnets.

....

....

....

13.2 Investigating magnetic fields

This challenge task relates to **13.3 Magnetic field patterns** from the Coursebook.

> In this challenge task, you will draw magnetic field patterns for fields of different strengths. You will then consider the plan of an investigation and suggest an improvement to the investigation.

A horseshoe magnet is like a bar magnet that is curved.

1 Draw, on the diagram, the magnetic field pattern for the horseshoe magnet.

> Draw lines to show the field pattern. Include arrows on the lines to show the direction of the field.

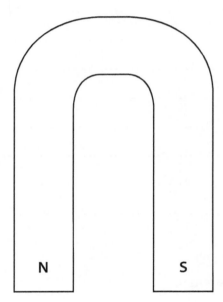

N   S

This diagram shows the outline of two bar magnets.

One of the magnets is **stronger** than the other.

The magnets are well separated, so they do **not** affect one another.

2 Draw the magnetic field pattern around each magnet.

> Your patterns should show the difference in strength between the two magnets.

N
S

stronger magnet

S
N

weaker magnet

Sam wants to investigate how a magnetic field passes through different materials. He has wood, paper, plastic, cotton and card.

He uses clamps to hold the bar magnet and the material to be investigated.

He then counts how many paper clips the magnet will support through the material.

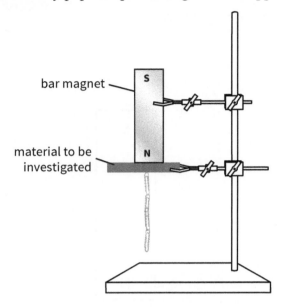

3 Write down the **dependent** and the **independent** variables in this investigation.

a dependent ....

b independent ....

4 Write down **two** variables that Sam must keep constant during this investigation.

....

....

5 Sam finds that the magnet will support the same number of paper clips though the wood and the plastic.

Explain how he could check whether the magnetic field really is passing through both these materials in exactly the same way.

....

....

....

....